On Earth

———

Also by Robert Creeley

Poetry
For Love
Words
The Charm
Pieces
A Day Book
Hello: A Journal
Later
Mirrors
Memory Gardens
Windows
Echoes
Life & Death
If I were writing this

Fiction
The Gold Diggers
The Island
Presences
Mabel: A Story

Drama
Listen

Essays
A Quick Graph: Collected Notes & Essays
  (edited by Donald M. Allen)
Was That a Real Poem & Other Essays
Autobiography
Tales out of School
Day Book of a Virtual Poet

Collections and Selections

The Collected Poems of Robert Creeley, 1945–1975

Selected Poems

So There: Poems, 1976–1983

Just in Time: Poems, 1984–1994

The Collected Essays of Robert Creeley

Collected Prose

As Editor

The Black Mountain Review (1954–1957)

New American Story (with Donald M. Allen)

Selected Writings of Charles Olson

Whitman: Selected Poems

The Essential Burns

Charles Olson: Selected Poems

George Oppen: Selected Poems

On Earth

Last Poems and an Essay

Robert Creeley

University of California Press
Berkeley   Los Angeles   London

University of California Press, one of the most distinguished university presses
in the United States, enriches lives around the world by advancing scholarship in
the humanities, social sciences, and natural sciences. Its activities are supported
by the UC Press Foundation and by philanthropic contributions from individuals
and institutions. For more information, visit www.ucpress.edu.

University of California Press
Berkeley and Los Angeles, California

University of California Press, Ltd.
London, England

The essay "Reflections on Whitman in Age" was first published in the
Virginia Quarterly Review 81, no. 2 (spring 2005). The manuscript page
from Walt Whitman, "Last of Ebb, and Daylight Waning," appears courtesy
of the Yale Collection of American Literature, Beinecke Rare Book and
Manuscript Library.

The lines from the poem "The Descent," by William Carlos Williams from
Collected Poems, 1939–1962, volume 2, copyright © 1948, 1962 by William
Carlos Williams. Reprinted by permission of New Directions Publishing
Corp. and Carcanet Press Limited.

Frontispiece: Robert Creeley in Marfa, Texas (late March 2005). Photograph
by Penelope Creeley.

Library of Congress Cataloging-in-Publication Data

Creeley, Robert, 1926–2005.
  On earth : last poems and an essay / Robert Creeley.
      p.   cm.
  ISBN 0-520-24791-4 (cloth : alk. paper)
    I. Title.

PS3505.R43O52 2006
811'.54—dc22   2005056873

Printed in Canada

15   14   13   12   11   10   09   08   07   06
10   9   8   7   6   5   4   3   2

The paper used in this publication meets the minimum requirements of
American National Standard for Information Sciences—Permanence of
Paper for Printed Library Materials, ANSI Z39.48–1984.

The publisher gratefully acknowledges the generous contribution to this book provided by the Humanities Endowment Fund of the University of California Press Foundation.

Contents

Poems

Essay

Poems

When I think

When I think of where I've come from
or even try to measure as any kind of
distance those places, all the various
people, and all the ways in which I re-
member them, so that even the skin I
touched or was myself fact of, inside,
could see through like a hole in the wall
or listen to, it must have been, to what
was going on in there, even if I was still
too dumb to know anything—When I think
of the miles and miles of roads, of meals,
of telephone wires even, or even of water
poured out in endless streams down streaks
of black sky or the dirt roads washed clean,
or myriad, salty tears and suddenly it's spring
again, or it was—Even when I think again of
all those I treated so poorly, names, places,
their waiting uselessly for me in the rain and
I never came, was never really there at all,
was moving so confusedly, so fast, so driven
like a car along some empty highway passing,
passing other cars—When I try to think of
things, of what's happened, of what a life is
and was, my life, when I wonder what it meant,

the sad days passing, the continuing, echoing deaths,
all the painful, belligerent news, and the dog still
waiting to be fed, the closeness of you sleeping, voices,
presences, of children, of our own grown children,
the shining, bright sun, the smell of the air just now,
each physical moment, passing, *passing,* it's what
it always is or ever was, just then, just there.

"To think . . ."

To think oneself again
into a tiny hole of self
and pull the covers round
and close the mouth—

shut down the eyes and hands,
keep still the feet,
and think of nothing if one can
not think of it—

a space in whose embrace
such substance is,
a place of emptiness
the heart's regret.

World's mind is after all
an afterthought
of what was there before
and is there still.

Old Song

I'm feeling ok still in some small way.
I've come too far to just go away.
I wish I could stay here some way.

So that what now comes wouldn't only be more
of what's to be lost. What's left would still leave more
to come if one didn't rush to get there.

What's still to say? Your eyes, your hair, your smile,
your body sweet as fresh air, your voice in the clear morning
after another night, *another night,* we lay together, sleeping?

If that has to go, it was never here.
If I know still you're here, then I'm here too
and love you, *and love you.*

For Ric, who Loved this World

The sounds
of his particular

music keep echoing,
stay in the soft

air months after
all's gone to

grass, to lengthening
shadows, to slanting

sun on shifting water,
to the late light's edges

through tall trees—
despite the mind's

still useless,
ponderous thought.

Oh, do you remember . . .

Remember sweet Ed
who despite being dead
embedded
all he said

with lead
could make you dead
too if that's it
for you,

oh dummy
of text,
be it western or mex?
He had grace like a swallow's,

nothing unfallow,
"Elizabethan" at root
with sideburns to boot,
quick on trigger,

also with jigger,
kept an apt time,
walked with a rhyme.
I loved his style

and his guile,
no friend to the loser,
vapid day cruiser,
elsewise bamboozler.

My Ed was quondam god
from human sod
who spoke not loud
but always clear and proud,

often with acid edge—
his pledge
to keep the faith
stays constant to this day.

Paul

I'll never forgive myself for the
violence propelled me at sad Paul
Blackburn, pushed in turn by both
our hopeless wives who were spitting
venom at one another in the heaven
we'd got ourselves to, Mallorca, mid-fifties,
where one could live for peanuts while
writing great works and looking at the
constant blue sea, etc. Why did I fight such
surrogate battles of existence with such
a specific friend as he was for sure?
Our first meeting NYC 1950 we talked two
and a half days straight without leaving the
apartment. He knew Auden and Yeats
by heart and had begun on Pound's lead
translating the Provençal poets, and was
studying with Moses Hadas at NYU. How
sweet this thoughtful beleaguered vulnerable
person whose childhood was full of New
England abusive confusion, his mother the too
often absent poet, Frances Frost! I wish
he were here now, we could go on talking,

I'd have company of my own age in this
drab burned out trashed dump we call the
phenomenal world where he once walked
the wondrous earth and knew its pleasures.

Mediterranean I

This same inexhaustible sea with impenetrable
Same blue look I stepped into when so young I
Had no reason for a life more than to hold on to
The one I had, wife, daughter, and two sons, older,
If seven and five, just, can be measure of more than
A vulnerable innocence. The back wheel of bike,
When brake failed, caught elder son's heel and used
It to stop, stripping the skin off almost to the bone.
I packed the place with ointment and bandaged it, not
Wanting to see how bad it might be, and for days son
Went on hop and hand holds spider fashion until,
Blessedly, it was well again. Oh life, oh miracle of
Day to day existence, sun, food and others! Would
Those who lived with me then believe how much
I loved them? Know how dumbly, persistently, I cared?

Mediterranean II

The cranky low decked freighter with orange stickup
stern cabin we could see from the open window of
this place each day out there on proverbial ocean has
moved away, shifting the focus of that blue to an
implacable distance now going out to a shaded, faded
edge of sky beyond all recalled dreams or places. One
so wanted it to be the old time story of them waiting till
dark at last came and then, with muffled oars, they'd row
into the hidden cove, climb up the adjoining cliff, and
into my waiting heart. How many times so long ago I'd
see the fisherman at nightfall row out into the darkened
sea with their long awkward boats, oars in unison, to what
determined fate, and if there were a world at edge of this
one, there at last they might pull ashore. Now the sea's slur-
ring, recurring sound, its battering, white capped, upon the
rocks, forces both free and unknown to me, have no work
but this tedious recurrence, dreams repeated, insistent, useless.

War

Blur of world is red smear on white page,
metaphors useless, thoughts impotent,
even the sense of days is lost
in the raging militance.

No life other than political,
the fact of family and friends
subjorned to the general
conduct of this bitter abstract.

I look in the mirror
to see old man looking back,
eyes creased, squinting,
finds nothing left.

He longs for significance,
a scratch in the dust, an odor
of some faint fruit, some flower
whose name he'd lost.

Why would they hate him
who fight now insistently
to kill one another
—why not.

Talking

I was trying to think of when rightly
to enter the conversation with all
the others talking thoughtfully,
comfortably. There was no occasion
to say that thirty years in the army was
a long time or that very probably the
world is flatter than one thinks. A star
is as far as one's eye can see? My shirt
had broken buttons I had hid with
my tie. Otherwise I was clean and
reasonably dressed. Yet, impatient to
join in, I could hear my voice landing
suddenly on the edge of another's com-
ment, me saying I can't now remember
what, just their saying, "What? What?"

Bye and Bye

Faded in face of apparent reality—
As it comes, I see it still goes on and on,
and even now still sitting at this table
is the smiling man who nobody seems to know.

Older, the walls apparently get higher.
No one seemingly gets to look over
to see the people pointing at the sky
where the old planes used to fly over.

I packed my own reality in a bag
and pushed it under the table,
thinking to retrieve it when able
some time bye and bye.

For John Wieners

Glass roses or something else hardly expected—an
Abundance of good will, a kind hand in usual troubles.
Do you hear voices all around you, a sort of whispering,
Echoing silence as if someone had left a window open?

Reading those several times with John, we were first
In a great hall, the Y uptown, where he said he'd
   heard Auden
Read, and now we did—the great velvet curtains,
   the useful
Sense of a company in the same place where we now
   stood, echoing.

Then at Bard, first time I'd met Tom Meyer still a
   student, and
We, John, Bobbie and me, had driven up from New York
   together,
In bleak aftermath of Olson's telling John he was going off
   with Panna,
On the phone in the Chelsea, the blasted heath we were
   leaving behind.

Sweet, you might say, impeccable gentleman, like Claude
   Rains, his

Boston accent held each word a particular obligation
   and value.
I see his face as still a young man, in San Francisco,
   hearing him
Talking with Joanne, hearing him talk with Joe Dunn,
   with friends.

When you are a poet as he was, you have no confusions,
   you write
The words you are given to, you are possessed or protected
   by a vision.
We are not going anywhere, we are somewhere, here where
   John is,
Where he's brought us much as he might himself this
   evening, to listen.

I think of all the impossible loves of my life, all the edges
   of feeling,
All the helpless reach to others one tried so bitterly to
   effect, to reach
As one might a hilltop, an edge of sea where the waves can
   break at last
On the shore. I think of just jumping into darkness, into
   deep water,

Into nothing one can ever point to as a place out there,
    just its shadow, a
Beckoning echo of something, a premonition, which does
    not warn but invites.
There is music in pain but not because of it, love in each
    persistent breath.
His was the Light of the World, a lit match or the whole
    city, burning.

After School

We'd set off into the woods
and would climb trees there
and throw things, shouting
at one another, great shrieking
cries I remember—or would, if
I dreamt—in dreams. *In dreams,*
the poet wrote, *begin responsibilities.*
I thought that was like going to
some wondrous place and all was
waiting there just for you to come
and do what had to be done.

Help!

Help's easy enough
If it comes in time.
Nothing's that hard
If you want to rhyme.

It's when they shoot you
It can hurt,
When the bombs blast off
And you're gone with a squirt.

Sitting in a bunker,
Feeling blue?
Don't be a loser,
It wasn't you

Wasn't you wanted
To go kill people,
Wasn't you caused
All this trouble.

I can't say, Run!
And I can't say, Hide!
But I still feel
What I feel inside.

It's wrong to kill people
Just to make them pay.
Wrong to blast cities
To make them go away.

You can't take everything
Away from fathers,
Mothers, babies,
Sisters and brothers.

You live in a house?
Wipe your feet!
Take a look around—
Ain't it neat

To come home at night
And have a home,
Be able to sit down
Even all alone?

You think that anyone
Ought to get pushed,
Shoved around
for some old Bush?

Use your head,
Don't get scared,
Stand up straight,
Show what you're made of.

America's heaven,
Let's keep it that way
Which means not killing,
Not running scared,

Not being a creep,
Not wanting to get "them."
Take a chance
And see what they want then.

Maybe just to be safe,
Maybe just to go home,
Maybe just to live
Not scared to the bone,

Not dumped on by world
They won't let you into,
Not forgotten by all
The ones who did it to you.

Sing together!
Make sure it's loud!
One's always one,
But the world's a crowd

Of people, people,
All familiar.
Take a look!
At least it won't kill you.

Shimmer

for Graham Dean

. . . We will all survive, addressed to such glimmering
shimmering transience with its insistent

invitation of other.
So close, so warm, so full.

I

At the edge of the evening then, at
the edge of the river, this edge

of being, as one says, one's own
given body, inexorable *me,* whatever then

can enter, what other stays there, initial,
wave of that changing weather, wind

lifting off sea, cloud fading northward,
even one's own hands' testament, clenched

seeming fists—*pinch me, pinch
ME* . . . The person inside the mirror

was hiding, came forward only
as you did, was too far inside you, too

much yourself doubling, twinned,
spun in image as you were, a patient

reality to provoke simple witness,
precluded, occluded, still cloudy.

I am going now
and you can't come with me . . .

There is no one here but you.
But who are you, who is it

one takes as life, as so-called reality,
like the mirror's shimmering light

as the sun strikes it, cobwebbed with dust,
layered with its own substance?

Oneself is instance, an echo
mirrored, doubled. Oneself is twin.

II

Looking in, you saw
a faint head there

at some end of what seemed
a mass of things, a layered

density of reflection, which was substance,
someone. Someone looking back.

But no one looked out.
All echo? Semblance?

No self to come home to,
no one to say, *be yourself*—to say, *it's you?*

There is no looking back
or way of being separate.

One can only stand there, *here,* apart
and see another *I* still, wherever, inside oneself.

Sad Walk

I've come to the old echoes again,
know it's where I've been before,
see the same old sun.

But backwards, from all the yesterdays,
it's still the same way,
who gets and who pays.

I was younger then,
walking along still open,
young and having fun.

But now it's just a sad walk
to an empty park,
to sit down and wait, wait to get out.

Caves

So much of my childhood seems
to have been spent in rooms—
at least in memory, the shades

pulled down to make it darker, the
shaft of sunlight at the window's edge.
I could hear the bees then gathering

outside in the lilacs, the birds chirping
as the sun, still high, began to drop.
It was summer, in heaven of small town.

hayfields adjacent, creak and croak
of timbers, of house, of trees, dogs,
elders talking, the lone car turning some

distant corner on Elm Street
way off across the broad lawn.
We dug caves or else found them,

down the field in the woods. We had
shacks we built after battering
at trees, to get branches, made tepee-

like enclosures, leafy, dense and in-
substantial. Memory is the cave
one finally lives in, crawls on

hands and knees to get into.
If Mother says, don't draw
on the book pages, don't color

that small person in the picture, then
you don't unless compulsion, distraction
dictate and you're floating off

on wings of fancy, of persistent seeing
of what's been seen here too, right here,
on this abstracting page. Can I use the green,

when you're done? What's that supposed to be,
says someone. All the kids crowd closer
in what had been an empty room

where one was trying at least
to take a nap, stay quiet, to think
of nothing but oneself.

*

Back into the cave, folks,
and this time we'll get it right?

Or, uncollectively perhaps, it was
a dark and stormy night he

slipped away from the group, got
his mojo working and before

you know it had that there
bison fast on the wall of the outcrop.

I like to think they thought,
though they seemingly didn't, at least

of something, like, where did X put the bones,
what's going to happen next, did she, he or it

really love me? Maybe that's what dogs are for,
but there's no material surviving

pointing to dogs as anyone's best friend, alas.
Still here we are no matter, still hacking away,

slaughtering what we can find to, leaving
far bigger footprints than any old mastodon.

You think it's funny? To have prospect
of being last creature on earth or at best a

company of rats and cockroaches?
You must have a good sense of humor!

Anyhow, have you noticed how everything's
retro these days? Like, something's been here before—

or at least that's the story. *I* think one picture is worth
a thousand words and I *know* one cave fits all sizes.

*

Much like a fading off airplane's
motor or the sound of the freeway

at a distance, it was all here clearly enough
and no one goes lightly into a cave,

even to hide. But to make such things
on the wall, against such obvious

limits, to work in intermittent dark,
flickering light not even held steadily,

all those insistent difficulties.
They weren't paid to, not that we know of,

and no one seems to have forced them.
There's a company there, tracks

of all kinds of people, old folks
and kids included. Were they having

a picnic? But so far in it's hardly
a casual occasion, flat on back with

the tools of the trade necessarily
close at hand. Try lying in the dark

on the floor of your bedroom and roll
so as you go under the bed and

ask someone to turn off the light.
Then stay there, until someone else comes.

Or paint up under on the mattress the last
thing you remember, dog's snarling visage

as it almost got you, or just what you do
think of as the minutes pass.

*

Hauling oneself through invidious
strictures of passage, the height
of the entrance, the long twisting
cramped passage, mind flickers, a lamp
lit flickers, lets image project
what it can, what it will, see there
war as wanting, see life as a river,
see trees as forest, family as
others, see a moment's respite,

hear the hidden bird's song, goes
along, goes along constricted, self-
hating, imploded, drags forward
in imagination of more, has no
time, has hatred, terror, power.
No light at the end of the tunnel.

*

The guide speaks of music, the
stalactites, stalagmites making a
possible xylophone, and some
Saturday night-like hoedown
businesses, what, every three
to four thousand years? One
looks and looks and time
is the variable, the determined
as ever river, lost on the way,
drifted on, laps and continues.
The residuum is finally silence,
internal, one's own mind constricted
to focus like any old camera
fixed in its function.

Like all good questions,
this one seems without answer,
leaves the so-called human
behind. It makes its own way
and takes what it's found
as its own and moves on.

*

It's time to go to bed
again, shut the light off,
settle down, straighten
the pillow and try to sleep.
Tomorrow's another day
and that was all thousands
and thousands of years ago,
myriad generations, even
the stones must seem changed.

The gaps in time,
the times one can't account for,
the practice it all took
even to make such images,

the meanings still unclear
though one recognizes
the subject, something has
to be missed, overlooked.

No one simply turns on a light.
Oneself becomes image.
The echo's got in front,
begins again what's over
just at the moment it was done.
No one can catch up, find
some place he's never been to
with friends he never had.

This is where it connects,
not meaning anything one
can know. This is where
one goes in and that's what's to find
beyond any thought or habit,
an arched, dark space, the rock,
and what survives of what's left.

Absence

Sun on the edges of leaves,
patterns of absent pleasure,
all that it meant
now gathered together.

Days all was away
and the clouds were far off
and the sky was heaven itself,
one wanted to stay

alone forever perhaps
where no one was,
and here again it is
still where it was.

The Ball

Room for one and all
around the gathering ball,
to hold the sacred thread,
to hold and wind and pull.

Sit in the common term.
All hands now move as one.
The work continues on.
The task is never done.

Which Way

Which one are you
and who would know.
Which way
would you have come this way.

And what's behind,
beside, before.
If there are more,
why are there more.

On Earth

One's here
and there is still elsewhere
along some road to hell
where all is well—

or heaven
even
where all the saints still wait
and guard the golden gate.

Saying Something

If, as one says, one says
something to another,
does it go on and on then
without apparent end?

Or does it only become talk,
balked by occasion, stopped
because it never got started,
was said to no one?

The Red Flower

What one thinks to hold
Is what one thinks to know,
So comes of simple hope
And leads one on.

The others there the same
With no one then to blame
These flowered circles handed.
So each in turn was bonded.

There the yellow bees will buzz,
And eyes and ears appear
As listening, witnessing hearts
Of each who enters here.

Yet eyes were closed—
As if the inside world one chose
To live in only as one knows.
No thing comes otherwise.

Walk on, on crippled leg,
Because one stumped with cane,
Turned in and upside down
As with all else, bore useless weight.

The way from here is there
And back again, from birth to death,
From egg to echo, flesh to eyeless skull.
One only sleeps to breathe.

The hook, the heart, the body
Deep within its dress, the folds of feelings,
Face to face to face, no bandaged simple place,
No wonder more than this, none less.

The Puzzle

Insoluble.
Neither one nor the other.
A wall.
An undulating water.

A weather.
A point in space.
Waste of time.
Something missed.

The faces.
Trees.
The unicorn
with its horn.

Able
as ready.
Fixed on heart
on head's prerogative.

Which way to go
up down
backward
forward.

In the sky
stars flash by.
Boats
head for heaven.

Down below
the pole
thrusts up
into the diamond.

Found, fills
its echo.
A baby.
Sound.

A Full Cup

Age knows little other than its own complaints.
Times past are not to be recovered ever.
The old man and woman are left to themselves.

When I was young, there seemed little time.
I hurried from day to day as if pursued.
Each thing I discovered, another came to possess me.

Love I could ask no questions of, it was nothing
I ever anticipated, ever thought would be mine.
Even now I wonder if it will escape me.

What I did, I did finally because I had to,
whether from need of my own or that of others
It is finally impossible to live and work only for pay.

I do not know where I've come from or where I am going.
Life is like a river, a river without beginning or end.
It's been my company all my life, its wetness, its insistent
    movement.

The only wisdom I have is what someone must have
    told me,

neither to take nor to give more than can be simply
   managed.
A full cup carried from the well.

Old Story

from The Diary of Francis Kilvert

One bell wouldn't ring loud enough.
So they beat the bell to hell, Max,
with an axe, show it who's boss,
boss. Me, I dreamt I dwelt in
some place one could relax
but I was wrong, wrong, *wrong.*
You got a song, man, sing it.
You got a bell, man, ring it.

Later (Wrightsville Beach)

Crusoe again, confounded, confounding purposes,
cruising, looking around for edges of the familiar,
the places he was in back then,

wherever, all the old sand and water.
How much he thought to be there he can't remember.
Shipwreck wasn't thinkable at least until

after it happened, and then he began at the edge,
the beach, going forward, backward, until he found
    place again.
Even years slipped past in the background.

The water, waves, sand, backdrop of the houses,
all changed now by the locals, the tourists,
whoever got there first and what they could make of it.

But his story is real too, the footprint, the displacement
when for the first time another is there, not just imagined,
and won't necessarily agree with anything, won't go away.

Dover Beach (Again)

The waves keep at it,
Arnold's Aegean Sophocles heard,
the swell and ebb,
the cresting and the falling under,

each one particular and the same—
Each day a reminder, each sun in its world, each face,
each word something one hears
or someone once heard.

Echo

Walking, the way it used to be,
talking, thinking—being in,
on the way—days after anything
went or came, with no one,
someone, having or not having a way.
What's a life if you look at it,
what's a hat if it doesn't fit.

Wish

I am
transformed into a clam.

I will
be very, very still.

So natural be,
and never 'me'

alone so far from home
a stone

would end it all
but for this tall

enduring tree,
the sea,

the sky
and I.

Here

Up a hill and down again.
Around and in—

Out was what it was all about
but now it's done.

At the end was the beginning,
just like it said or someone did.

Keep looking, keep looking,
keep looking.

TO MY/LITTLE:
PEN'S
VALENTINE

To My
Little

Dear
Yo
Wh
Fr

Do *better*
To
Where
From

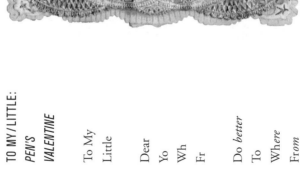

Dear (begin again)

Yo(u)

W(ere my)

Fr(iend)

To My
Little To

My
Love

Valentine for You

Where from, where to
the thought to do—

Where with, whereby
the means themselves now lie—

Wherefor, wherein
such hopes of reconciling heaven—

Even the way is changed
without you, even the day.

Essay

Reflections on Whitman in Age

> The descent beckons
>   as the ascent beckoned.
>   Memory is a kind
> of accomplishment,
>   a sort of renewal
>   even
> an initiation, since the spaces it opens are new places
>   inhabited by hordes
>   heretofore unrealized . . .
>
>   W. C. Williams, "The Descent"

In age one is oneself reflective, both of what it has been to live and of what that act has become as a resonance (I'd almost written a *residence*) in memory—what it all meant, so to speak, what it had felt like. It is very hard for me to believe that what William Carlos Williams calls "the descent" (to the ending of life, one must presume) can ever be more than the accumulation a literal life must be fact of, the *substance* of a body, the *history* of such body in a particular time and place, the *manifest* of that locating "thing" in the myriad ways in which it has engaged and been engaged by the world surrounding.

Yet even the "world" itself is imagination, simply "the length of a human life," as its etymology defines. The one hundred and fifty years since Whitman's *Leaves of Grass* was first published is a moment in any world so conceived, and the bridges to and from such world are not determined by rational judgments or understanding. One *knows,* as is said—one *recognizes* the footprints on the floor of the caves in the Dordogne, dating back to the Upper Paleolithic—so very far, finally, from any intellectual understanding or resolution, however insistently attempted.

Poetry is of such "age" and carries with it the same character of echo. One does not hear it unless in the most obvious way one listens. Otherwise its correspondences and determined intimacies of feeling—all the physical reception that being human constitutes—are lost. Now I know, for example, that age itself is a *body,* not a measure of time or record of how much one has grown. So Williams told me years ago, speaking of himself. "You reach for it but you cannot quite get it. You try but you fail."

In a Women's Studies class in Warsaw, of all places, I asked the students, both men and women, what was their sense of old people? I had been reading almost obsessively Simone de Beauvior's *Old Age* (*La Vieillesse,* 1970). "They don't smell good," one answered. "They ramble on." "They can't take care of themselves. No one understands what they're talking about, and they look awful." I wanted to insist, "But you will all grow old, at least if you have any luck. To be human has growing old at its end . . ." How could they possibly hear me—and how abstract, finally, that aged world must be for them—even the literally smelly elders and their mindless wandering battle must seem altogether without reality. What to say? Walt Whitman, some three years before his death, wrote this poem, among others.

The touch of flame—the illuminating fire—the loftiest look at
    last,
O'er city, passion, sea—o'er prairie, mountain, wood—the earth
    itself;
The airy, different, changing hues of all, in falling twilight,
Objects and groups, bearings, faces, reminiscences;
The calmer sight—the golden setting, clear and broad;
So much i' the atmosphere, the points of view, the situations
    whence we scan,
Bro't out by them alone—so much (perhaps the best) unreck'd
    before;
The lights indeed from them—old age's lambent peaks.

                    "Old Age's Lambent Peaks," 1888

The common sense is that Whitman's poems faded as he grew older, that their art grew more mechanical and that the poems themselves had rarely the power of his more youthful writing. The life, however, is finally the poetry, the issue and manifest of its existence—not as some mystic aspect of vision or of surreal realms of elsewhere, but literally so—just as Keats's "mortal hand still capable of grasping." I want to ask, Where does one think this man *is*—other than watching the sunset? Where is this place wherein there is "The airy, different, changing hues of all, in falling twilight, / Objects and groups, bearings, faces, reminiscences; / The calmer sight." What are the compulsions of the cadence, the "airy, different" rhythms? Why the persistent backbeat, the "falling twilight," the "objects and groups, bearings, faces, reminiscences . . ."

For a poet these details are profound masteries in themselves and speak as emphatically as will the evident content one otherwise calls "the meaning." Whitman seems as if writing with a habit so deep and familiar it no longer separates from him as an art or intention. Rather, it sounds out as does "Bare ruined choirs, where late the sweet birds sang . . ." But Whitman is older, and therefore wiser, than was Shakespeare in so writing. Here is perhaps a better parallel:

There's a certain Slant of light,
Winter Afternoons—
That oppresses, like the Heft
Of Cathedral Tunes—

Heavenly Hurt, it gives us—
We can find no scar,
But internal difference,
Where the Meanings, are—

None may teach it—Any—
'Tis the Seal Despair—
An imperial affliction
Sent us of the Air—

When it comes, the Landscape listens—
Shadows—hold their breath—
When it goes, 'tis like the Distance
On the look of Death—

"There's a certain Slant of light,"
The Complete Poems of Emily Dickinson,
ed. Thomas H. Johnson, 1960

No metric will quite serve to explain Emily Dickinson's rhythms here, though the frame is certainly an old one. What, then, is one reading—or hearing—in the insistent

"Where the Meanings, are," and how accommodate "When it comes, the Landscape listens—/ Shadows—hold their breath—," etc.? It cannot be a didactic "intelligence" calling such sounds to order. All one is, is a body. So it is that which speaks first.

Yet poetry is still thought of, insistently, as a product, as something answering either to a determined definition or else to a use not necessarily its own. Gregory Corso rightly said that only the poet can validate him- or herself. There is no other reference or judgment that can give more than an opinion. Opinions are rightly and generously the response an art may depend upon, but they do not determine what it is or can be.

"The poet thinks with his poem," Williams wrote. "In that lies his thought." What Whitman was thinking in age is not much different from that "thought" by all people in a similar situation. The titles he uses for the various later sections of *Leaves of Grass* are good instances: "Autumn Rivulets," "Whispers of Heavenly Death," "From Noon to Starry Night," "Songs of Parting, Sands at Seventy (*First Annex*)," and "Good-Bye My Fancy (*Second Annex*)." One thinks of the persistent, familiar framing of life implied—or, as put by then-youthful John Ashbery, "How much longer will I be able to inhabit the divine sepulcher . . ." Whatever, the end seems never far enough away.

It's "Fancy" that's most useful to me here, the key, as it were, to all that did take and find place, all that world and what Whitman or any of us did make of it. It's a great word in itself, the contraction of *fantasy*: "c. 1325, 'illusory appearance,' from O.Fr. *fantasie,* from L. *phantasia,* from Gk. *phantasia* 'appearance, image, perception, imagination,' from *phantazesthai* 'picture to oneself,' from *phantos* 'visible,' from *phainesthai* 'appear,' in late Gk. 'to imagine, have visions,' related to *phaos, phos* 'light.' Sense of 'whimsical notion, illusion' is pre-1400, followed by that of 'imagination,' which is first attested 1539. Sense of 'day-dream based on desires' is from 1926, as is *fantasize.* . . ." (The year I was born!) "Reality" is the given *imago mundi,* the *fantasy* into which one is born. It's where thought and sense find a way of meeting—and in no one more vividly than in Whitman. "Good-Bye My Fancy" (1891, the first of two late poems that use this phrase for title) is a painful, displacing recognition:

Good-bye my fancy—(I had a word to say,
But 'tis not quite the time—The best of any man's word or say,

Is when its proper place arrives—and for its meaning,
I keep mine till the last.)

It is a loss age itself determines, which parentheses cannot change. One knows all too well that what's to be said has only its own occasion. I think of Yeats writing "Sailing to Byzantium" (1927), beginning to feel the insistent, nagging limits of a physical body. But it is a controlled reflection, almost elegant in its securing urbanity:

O sages standing in God's holy fire
As in the gold mosaic of a wall
Come from the holy fire, perne in the gyre,
And be the singing masters of my soul.
Consume my heart away; sick with desire
And fastened to a dying animal
It knows not what it is; and gather me
Into the artifice of eternity.

Three years later, now markedly ill, he writes in the active apprehension of death a very different poem:

The unpurged images of day recede;
The Emperor's drunken soldiery are abed;

Night resonance recedes, night-walkers' song
After great cathedral gong;
A starlit or a moonlit dome disdains
All that man is,
All mere complexities,
The fury and the mire of human veins.

"Byzantium," 1930

The metaphors here ground in the all-too-actual, the clock's physical striking, the edges of the day's thinking still insistent as the sounds of persons moving in the street below now fade and grow quiet. So he lies there waiting, necessarily passive, in a world no longer in any sense his own.

Whitman is characteristically reported as physically vulnerable, beginning with his first stroke in his early fifties. He appears to have been a big man, but here is an account of his arrival at Morgan's Hall in Camden for his seventieth birthday celebration:

Whitman himself was not present when the crowd gathered at 5 P.M. [May 31, 1889]. . . . After dinner was cleared away, the air buzzed with anticipation of the poet's arrival. Soon a policeman cried, "He's coming!" The hall fell silent and all eyes were riveted on the entrance door.

Doubtless, many hearts sank at his pitiful condition. His large, once robust frame was now slumped in a wheel chair pushed by a male nurse. He had famously boasted in a poem of his perfect health, but a series of strokes—"whacks," he called them—had partly paralyzed him, while digestive and excretive disorders gave him what he described as a "soggy, wet, sticky" feeling as of tar oozing over him.

Still, the undeniable Whitman magnetism was there. He was wrapped in a blue overcoat, under which he wore a black dinner jacket, a natty departure from his usual plain gray one. His clean white shirt was open at the neck, and his round felt hat was pushed back on his head. His snowy hair and cascading beard gave him a jovian majesty. Tiny wrinkles seamed his face, but his pink complexion gave him a deceptive air of health. His gray-blue eyes, their large lids drooping, had a look of tired wisdom and stolid impassivity. The high-arched eyebrows made him seem slightly surprised.

David S. Reynolds, *Walt Whitman's America:*
A Cultural Biography, Prologue

A sequence of poems written a few years earlier, "Fancies at Navesink," makes most clear the fact of age and, particularly, how Whitman felt himself located in that circumstance. He had long practice in being the curious "icon" of his own intent. Borges says of him, "Walt Whitman himself was a myth, a myth of a man who wrote, a very unfortunate man, very lonely, and yet he made of himself a rather splendid vagabond. I have pointed out that Whitman is perhaps the only writer on earth who has managed to create a mythological person of himself and one of the three persons of the Trinity is the reader, because when you read Walt Whitman, you are Walt Whitman. Very strange that he did that, the only person on earth."

Although the ability to project such scale as "Song of Myself" lessens in age, Whitman's impulse and rhetoric stay put. So I wonder just when he had been on that high point of ground overlooking the Navesink River and the sea. He must have known, like they say, that a local name for "Navesink" was "Neversunk," come not as the former from the name of a tribe of the Lenni-Lenapi family, who cultivated oysters on the banks of the river, but from the fact that the hills, as the sun lowered, cast such long shadows out over the sea. So they were thought by passing ships "never" to be "sunk" out of sight. The rise of ground back of the river, Mount Mitchell, is the highest point on all the Atlantic Coast from Maine to Florida. So one looks out from it, whether in sight or in mind, and sees an ample and far-reaching prospect—sea, town, river, and sky. Whitman begins with an echo of nostalgic history:

The Pilot in the Mist

Steaming the northern rapids—(an old St. Lawrence
    reminiscence,
A sudden memory-flash comes back, I know not why,
Here waiting for the sunrise, gazing from this hill;)
Again 'tis just at morning—a heavy haze contends with
    day-break,
Again the trembling, laboring vessel veers me—I press through
    foam-dash'd rocks that almost touch me,
Again I mark where aft the small thin Indian helmsman
Looms in the mist, with brow elate and governing hand.

There is such pleasure here in the sounds of the words as
they move, "Again 'tis just at morning," "Again the trem-
bling, laboring vessel veers me." The markedly early hour is
lovely as well, dear to children and the old, with its fresh,
open quiet, its promptings unquestioned by anyone at all. I
am moved by the way the apparent real, "Here waiting for
this sunrise, gazing from this hill," melds with the recollec-
tion, the "foam-dashed rocks that almost touch me." Just so
the habit of giving directions in the town where I grew up
would say, "Turn left by the old house that used to be there
before it burned down." Does it matter, I wonder, that
Whitman may never have "steam[ed] the northern rapids,"

that there is no "old St. Lawrence reminiscence, / A sudden memory-flash"? I recognize increasingly in my own insistent memories that much they bring with them is both true and false. They have their own story.

The next section of "Fancies at Navesink" seems most a reckoning-up, an evidence of his models and ambitions, but it doesn't argue that they were his finally—"Tennyson's fair ladies, / Meter or wit the best," etc.

Had I the Choice

Had I the choice to tally greatest bards
To limn their portraits, stately, beautiful, and emulate at will,
Homer with all his wars and warriors—Hector, Achilles, Ajax,
Or Shakspere's woe-entangled Hamlet, Lear, Othello —
    Tennyson's fair ladies,
Meter or wit the best, or choice conceit to wield in perfect rhyme,
    delight of singers;
These, these, O sea, all these I'd gladly barter,
Would you the undulation of one wave, its trick to me transfer
Or breathe one breath of yours upon my verse,
And leave its odor there.

I suppose this is what poets can be persuaded they should write. Poems about writing poems are almost without exception drab. *Look at me, / I'm being sea!* But one recalls what he had done—as here:

. . .Whereto answering, the sea,
Delaying not, hurrying not,
Whisper'd me through the night, and very plainly before daybreak,
Lisp'd to me the low and delicious word death,
And again death, death, death, death
Hissing melodious, neither like the bird nor like my arous'd
    child's heart,
But edging near as privately for me rustling at my feet,
Creeping thence steadily up to my ears and laving me softly
    all over,
Death, death, death, death, death.

"Out of the Cradle Endlessly Rocking," 1859

In contrast, "Had I the Choice" presumes a choice, which is not so simply the case, as Whitman must have known. "These, these, O sea, all these I'd gladly barter" is no loss of powers, rather a curiously determined lapse, almost perversely "chosen" here. In contrast, he next tries a large cast, already familiar in his earlier work:

You Tides with Ceaseless Swell

You tides with ceaseless swell! you power that does this work!
You unseen force, centripetal, centrifugal, through space's spread,
Rapport of sun, moon, earth, and all the constellations,
What are the messages by you from distant stars to us? what
    Sirius'? what Capella's?
What central heart—and you the pulse—vivifies all? what
    boundless aggregate of all?
What subtle indirection and significance in you? what clue you?
    what fluid, vast identity,
Holding the universe with all its parts as one—as sailing in a ship?

Those last five words come in with such poignance. Like
Coleridge's "gentleman from Porlock," they break the slid-
ing rhetoric with such a charmingly apt instance of what
Whitman had in mind. Otherwise I have the feeling that this
section also is finally an exercise. The sea can't be put as such
a simplifying reference—it's too real.

If there has been any confusion as to what Whitman is
centered upon, it's now clear indeed that the sea is his pre-
occupation, as it has been persistently throughout his life. In
age the sea becomes more and more present as source and as
that to which one returns, metaphorically perhaps but also
quite literally, losing signifying name and function, entering

the utterly common fate of all beyond any differentiation or exception. There is no longer a locating ground.

Last of Ebb, and Daylight Waning

Last of ebb, and daylight waning,
Scented sea-cool landward making, smells of sedge and salt
    incoming,
With many a half-caught voice sent up from the eddies,
Many a muffled confession—many a sob and whisper'd word
As of speakers far or hid.

How they sweep down and out! How they mutter!
Poets unnamed—artists greatest of any, with cherish'd lost designs,
Love's unresponse—a chorus of age's complaints—hope's last
    words,
Some suicide's despairing cry, *Away to the boundless waste, and*
    never again return.

On to oblivion then!
On, on and do your part, ye burying, ebbing tide!
On for your time, ye furious debouché!

In the surviving manuscript of this poem one can see the same determining emphasis. Again it is useful evidence of Whitman's need to find the active *place* of his own situation, caught with neither a "here" nor a "there" to define him

Last of ebb and daylight

Last of ebb, and daylight waning.
Scented sea-breaths landward making —
smells of sedge and salt incoming,
With many a half-caught voice sent
up from the whirls and eddies.
Many a muffled confession — many a
sob and whisper'd word.
As of speakers far or hid.

How they sweep down and out! how they mutter!
Poets unnamed — poets and artists greatest of any
with all their lost design
Pride of lands — tones of the dying
Tones of the dying — a chorus of age's complaints —
love unreturn'd — hope's last words,
Some suicide's despairing beguiling cry. Away
to the boundless waste. and no more
again return.

On to oblivion then! on
On — on, and do your part ye shivering waters!
On, for your time, ye furious debouché!

securely. "Love's unresponse," for example, is not at all the same as "Love unreturned," apparently the initial phrase he thought to use. In the resolved draft "Love" is what no longer responds, simply does not answer. The distance from person increases as "love" shifts from agency, a state, to "Love," a generality, a subject having its own authority and determination. In like sense, the shift from "As from speakers" to "As of speakers" in the fifth line marks a very different human relation.

And Yet Not You Alone

And yet not you alone, twilight and burying ebb,
Nor you, ye lost designs alone—nor failures, aspirations;
I know, divine deceitful ones, your glamour's seeming;
Duly by you, from you, the tide and light again—duly the
    hinges turning
Duly the needed discord-parts offsetting, blending,
Weaving from you, from Sleep, Night, Death, itself,
The rhythmus of Birth eternal.

Now as ever the insistent wash, the roll and return of the waves, the light recurring, "duly the hinges turning" must be the constants, "the rhythmus of Birth eternal," writ however large. One *needs* them, needs the familiar, the company, the chittering birds at the feeder, the far-off hum of the persistent traffic, the chimneys and cranes out the window over the rooftops to the trashed small harbor.

Daily, it would seem, the persons one has lived with go, leaving an inexorable emptiness. Some bright person, writing of the old, remarked that their insistent rehearsal of who has died would be better understood if one thinks of old age as a neighborhood in which almost daily a house burns down. Who would not be affected by that, one wonders. Isn't that worth talking about?

Proudly the Flood Comes In

Proudly the flood comes in, shouting, foaming, advancing,
Long it holds at the high, with bosom broad outswelling,
All throbs, dilates —the farms, woods, streets of cities—
    workmen at work,
Mainsails, topsails, jibs, appear in the offing—steamers' pennants
    of smoke—and under the forenoon sun,
Freighted with human lives, gaily the outward bound, gaily the
    inward bound,
Flaunting from many a spar the flag I love.

No doubt Whitman was making himself convenient to public sentiment of the time, much as today one recognizes that not a single member of Congress will state him- or herself as *not* "believing in God." The "flaunting" of flags is hardly new, and who knows but Whitman's own sentiments were so persuaded? He surely loved a parade. But the poet, or, for my interests now, the "Dear old man," as Tennyson addressed him in a letter in 1887, the increasingly sick old man, is not so clearly present. This verse, despite its bright sense of physical details, is committed overly to a public display of his authority as classic "elder statesman."

Horace Traubel in his exceptional devotion to the recording of Whitman's last years, *With Walt Whitman in Camden* in nine volumes, has many reports of his poor health. Though Traubel wants his hero to win out, he is not expectably very confident. Here is what he writes as part of an entry, "Monday, June 4, 1888":

Ferguson referred to me this morning several questions about which I had to confer with W. I went to Camden in consequence this noon, reaching 328 [Mickle Street] at a quarter past twelve. Found Harned there with two of his children, Mrs. Davis also, all of them in the parlor, anxiously regarding W., who lay on the sofa. What was the matter? My alarm was instant. But W. was very cheerful: "I seem to have had since last night three strokes of a paralytic character—shocks, premonitions. That's all there is to it. Don't worry about it, boy." He held my hand warmly and firmly. When he drove off from Harned's yesterday with Doctor Bucke he was in great good humor and (for him) apparent health. In the evening he undertook to sponge himself, in his own room, alone, and while so engaged fell to the floor, finding himself unable to move or to call for assistance, lying there, he thought, helplessly, for several hours. When asked why he did not call Mrs. Davis he said: "I thought best to fight it out myself." He added to me: "I have had many such attacks in the past—they do not alarm me—though I am aware they do not signify good health." This morning two perhaps lighter attacks had followed—one of which, the last, that from which he was recovering on my arrival, having somewhat affected his speech. "I never suffered that entanglement in my former experiences," he explained. Harned was present when this occurred. No doctor there. "Don't get a doctor," commanded W., adding humorously: "I think of it this way, you know: that if the doctors come I shall not only have to fight the disease but fight them, whereas if I am left alone I have but the one foe to contend with." Mrs. Davis happening to say: "I hope it will all pass off," he replied: "I guess it will but if it does not it will be all right." W. attributes the trouble to his "infernal indigestion" suffered of late. "I have passed through hells of indigestion." Harned suggested: "Fast for awhile—cut your belly off." W. smiled. "I am aware of the need of caution but I am aware also of the fact that I must keep the fire going."

There's a kind of Will Rogers affability here given Whitman, as if he were being depicted primarily for his role of the Great Grey Poet rather than described as the old and vulnerable man he clearly was. It's no joke to be "several hours" on the floor, unable to raise oneself or to call for help.

Traubel seems the perfect straight man, however, for such phrases as "I have had many such attacks in the past—they do not alarm me—though I am aware they do not signify good health." What could Traubel have written, I suppose, no matter what Whitman said.

By That Long Scan of Waves

By that long scan of waves, myself call'd back, resumed upon
    myself,
In every crest some undulating light or shade—some retrospect,
Joys, travels, studies, silent panoramas—scenes, ephemeral,
The long past war, the battles, hospital sights, the wounded and
    the dead,
Myself through every by-gone phase—my idle youth—old age
    at hand,
My three score years of life summ'd up, and more, and past,
By any grand ideal tried, intentionless, the whole a nothing,
And haply yet some drop within God's scheme's ensemble—
    some wave, or part of a wave,
Like one of yours, ye multitudinous ocean.

Whitman's "call'd back" is quite other than Emily Dickinson's brief, last note to Louise and Fanny Norcross, sent shortly before her death, "Little Cousins, Called Back, Emily." One needs something wherewith to make place for whatever a life has been, its human summary if nothing else. Did it matter? Was it all phantasmagoria? Who was finally there? The roll and turn of the physical waves, their ceaseless repetition, the seeming return of each so particular, the same and yet not the same—this is the "call," recall (*recoil*), he has come to, an indeterminant spill of memories "By any grand ideal tried, intentionless, the whole a nothing." But one hopes to have been included even so, to have mattered, taken place, been part of, *done*—as one says in this utterly merciless country—*something*.

Then Last of All

Then last of all, caught from these shores, this hill,
Of you O tides, the mystic human meaning:
Only by law of you, your swell and ebb, enclosing me the same,
The brain that shapes, the voice that chants this song.

"Then Last of All," one tries to make sense of it, to get a grip on it, somehow find an enduring sense that the human has a sustaining pattern, is part of the proverbial whole. Age would seem age forever, but the years between Whitman's writing of these lines and my own words here mark so many bitter recognitions. I think of Robert Duncan's evocation of Whitman in "A Poem Beginning with a Line by Pindar":

. . . Hoover, Coolidge, Harding, Wilson
hear the factories of human misery turning out commodities.
For whom are the holy matins of the heart ringing?
Noble men in the quiet of morning hear
Indians singing the continent's violent requiem.
Harding, Wilson, Taft, Roosevelt,
idiots fumbling at the bride's door,
hear the cries of men in meaningless debt and war.
Where among these did the spirit reside
that restores the land to productive order?
McKinley, Cleveland, Harrison, Arthur,
Garfield, Hayes, Grant, Johnson,
dwell in the roots of the heart's rancor.
How sad "amid lanes and through old woods"
        echoes Whitman's love for Lincoln!

There is no continuity then. Only a few
        posts of the good remain. I too
that am a nation sustain the damage
        where smokes of continual ravage
obscure the flame.

            It is across great scars of wrong
        I reach toward the song of kindred men
        and strike again the naked string
old Whitman sang from. Glorious mistake!
        that cried:

"The theme is creative and has vista."
"He is the president of regulation."

I see always the under side turning,
fumes that injure the tender landscape.
     From which up break
lilac blossoms of courage in daily act
     striving to meet a natural measure.

The Opening of the Field, 1960

I could go on quoting. Age wants no one to leave. Things close down in age, like stores, like lights going off, like a world disappearing in a vacancy one had no thought might happen. It's no fun, no victory, no reward, no direction. One sits and waits, most usually for the doctor. So one goes inside oneself, as it were, looks out from that "height" with only imagination to give prospect. Albeit so bitterly young, John Keats could nonetheless write with exact clarity:

Adieu! the fancy cannot cheat so well
     As she is fam'd to do, deceiving elf.
Adieu! adieu! thy plaintive anthem fades
     Past the near meadows, over the still stream,
         Up the hill-side; and now 'tis buried deep
             In the next valley-glades:

Was it a vision, or a waking dream?
    Fled is that music—Do I wake or sleep?
        "Ode to a Nightingale," 1819

Perhaps Whitman's "fancy" was not only such a power but a person as well, even the memory of a person, that presence acknowledged over and over just as was his own being there too insistently emphasized always. In that world, perhaps one's whole life is a dream, a practical, peculiarly material dream, whose persons become the same complex "music" that Keats's nightingale evokes, a tenacious fabric of inexhaustible yearning. Is that the "world" that has to fall away in age? When one can no longer sustain it? Can it even matter, given—as the poet Edward Dorn made clear—the last thing a man says will be a word.

Good-bye my Fancy!
Farewell dear mate, dear love!
I'm going away, I know not where,
Or to what fortune, or whether I may ever see you again,
So Good-bye my Fancy.

Now for my last—let me look back a moment;
The slower fainter ticking of the clock is in me,
Exit, nightfall, and soon the heart-thud stopping.

Long have we lived, joy'd, caress'd together;
Delightful!—now separation—Good-bye my Fancy.

Yet let me not be too hasty,
Long indeed have we lived, slept, filter'd, become really—
    into one;
Then if we die we die together, (yes, we'll remain one,)
If we go anywhere we'll go together to meet what happens,
May-be we'll be better off and blither, and learn something,
May-be it is yourself now really ushering to the true songs,
    (who knows?)
May-be it is you the mortal knob really undoing, turning—so
    now finally,
Good-bye—and hail! my Fancy.

"Good-Bye My Fancy," 1891

Acknowledgments

Robert died at sunrise on March 30th, 2005, in Odessa, Texas.

The poems in this book were found in the black reading folder on his desk in Marfa, where he and I had been living since mid-February. Robert's habit was always to type out and print a poem after writing it. Then he would add it to this black folder and muse over it, look at its shape, and read it aloud again and again, both to himself and to me. He was testing the poems: trying them out, listening acutely, getting the feel of them.

The first part of this book is the contents of that black folder, pretty much as we found it.

The second part, the essay "Whitman in Age," was written over Christmas 2004. Robert worked at it intensely, with passion, delight, and often tears. He would disappear for hours to his desk upstairs here in Providence, peer out through the attic windows at the morsel of industrial harbor he could glimpse between the neighbors' shingled rooftops, listen to music and talk to himself. Later, after hours of work, he'd re-emerge satisfied, relaxed, and ready to celebrate with us.

Many people have helped make *On Earth* a reality; Will, Hannah, Sarah, and I are most grateful for all their help.

The Lannan Foundation's recognition of Robert's lifetime of literary achievement gave him peace and pleasure. Our residency in Marfa was also thanks to the Lannan Foundation. Their backup and help during that time was extraordinary and offered with exceptional courtesy.

The Liguria Study Center Bogliasco Foundation gave us a reflective six weeks on the Mediterranean.

Francesco Clemente's paintings, with which Robert felt deep rapport, gave him inspiration to write six of these poems: "The Ball," "Which Way," "On Earth," "Saying Something," "The Red Flower," and "The Puzzle."

"Caves" was written in June 2004 while we traveled in the Dordogne at the invitation of Clayton and Caryl Eshleman, on a trip sponsored by the Ringling School of Art and Design in Sarasota, Florida.

Laura Cerruti, Benjamin Friedlander, Peter Gizzi, and Elizabeth Willis have been crucial in making this book possible. Heartfelt thanks, too, to Michael Davidson, Raymond Foye, Forrest Gander, Susan Howe, Michael Gizzi, Vincent Katz, and C. D. Wright.

Ted Genoways, editor of *Virginia Quarterly Review,* has

been exceptionally helpful in preparing the text of "Whitman in Age" for publication. The essay first appeared in *Virginia Quarterly Review* 81, no. 2 (spring 2005).

"Caves" appeared in *Harvard Magazine* 108, no. 1 (September–October 2005) and will be published in a forthcoming issue of *Conjunctions*.

Other journals, institutions, and presses whose publications have included work in this book and to whom we extend our thanks are: *Ploughshares, Sirena: poesia, arte y critica,* Cuneiform Press, Thunder's Mouth Press/Nation Books, Paradigm Press, the Rose Art Museum, and the Stephen Lacey Gallery, London.

Penelope Creeley
Providence, Rhode Island
June 2005

Designer: Sandy Drooker
Text: 9.5/14 Adobe Garamond
Display: Akzidenz Grotesk
Compositor: BookMatters, Berkeley
Printer and Binder: Friesens Corporation